NINJAS

JAPAN'S STEALTHY SECRET AGENTS

By Matt Chandler
Illustrated by Silvio dB

Consultant:
Tim Solie
Adjunct Professor of History
Minnesota State University, Mankato
Mankato, Minnesota

DISCARD

CAPSTONE PRESS
a capstone imprint

Graphic Library is published by Capstone Press,
1710 Roe Crest Drive, North Mankato, Minnesota 56003
www.mycapstone.com

Library of Congress Cataloging-in-Publication data
Names: Chandler, Matt, author. | Silvio dB, illustrator.
Title: Ninjas : Japan's stealthy secret agents / by Matt Chandler ; illustrated by Silvio DB.
Description: North Mankato, Minnesota : Capstone Press, [2019] | Series: Graphic library.
   Graphic history: warriors | Includes bibliographical references and index. | Audience:
   Grades 4–6. | Audience: Ages 9–12.
Identifiers: LCCN 2018031869 (print) | LCCN 2018038873 (ebook) | ISBN 9781543555110
   (eBook PDF) | ISBN 9781543555035 (library binding) | ISBN 9781543559293 (paperback)
Subjects: LCSH: Ninja—Comic books, strips, etc.—Juvenile literature. | LCGFT: Comics
   (Graphic works)
Classification: LCC UB271.J3 (ebook) | LCC UB271.J3 C53 2019 (print) |
   DDC 355.5/48—dc23
LC record available at https://lccn.loc.gov/2018031869

Summary: In graphic novel format, tells several tales of legendary ninjas while exploring the
history, armor, weapons, and battles of these stealthy warriors from feudal Japan.

EDITOR
Aaron J. Sautter

ART DIRECTOR
Nathan Gassman

DESIGNER
Ted Williams

MEDIA RESEARCHER
Jo Miller

PRODUCTION SPECIALIST
Kathy McColley

Design Elements: Shutterstock: michelaubryphoto, Reinhold Leitner, Skocko

Printed and bound in the United states of America.
052019   001956

TABLE OF CONTENTS

Beginning in the late 1400s, a new kind of warrior emerged in Japan. Known as *shinobi*, ninja warriors acted as spies, thieves, and assassins in feudal Japan. It was a dangerous job. Only the bravest, most-skilled people could become true shinobi.

Ninjas were masters of stealth. They often wore dark clothes to travel and hide at night. Ninjas could even hide underwater. They would breathe through a bamboo tube while waiting to strike their target.

To become a shinobi required a lot of training. Most ninjas were poor Japanese farmers or lower-class citizens who were recruited to learn the martial art of *ninjutsu*.

I will train you to fight. In time you'll become fearless spies and masters of ninjutsu.

The soldiers are ready. We'll reach the village by nightfall and attack them while they sleep.

Ninjas were highly-trained in combat, but their main role was working as spies. Japanese lords often fought battles to control regions of land. They'd hire ninjas to steal information about their enemies.

I must get this news back to my lord so he can defend against the invasion!

Although they were stealthy, ninjas were sometimes discovered and had to fight. Ninjas were well-trained to use weapons and ninjutsu in combat. Still, many lost their lives in such battles.

ZZZING!

UGGGHH!

CLANG!

AAARGGH!

CHING!

The people of Japan often told stories about ninja warriors. Over time, the stories were exaggerated and ninjas became legendary figures.

Today nobody is certain how much truth remains in these old folktales. But the following stories show how legendary ninjas played a big part in Japan's history.

5

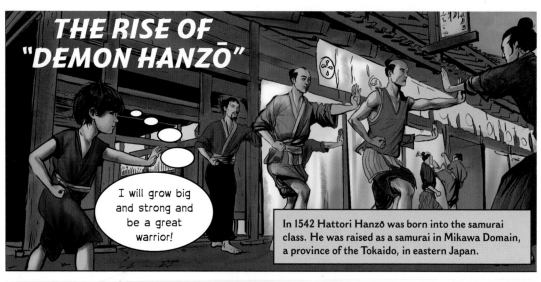

THE RISE OF "DEMON HANZŌ"

I will grow big and strong and be a great warrior!

In 1542 Hattori Hanzō was born into the samurai class. He was raised as a samurai in Mikawa Domain, a province of the Tokaido, in eastern Japan.

As Hanzō grew older he trained to be a ninja fighter. He practiced for many hours and grew to be a fierce warrior.

I must never give up. I will do whatever it takes to prove myself worthy of fighting for my people!

When he was 16-years-old, Hanzō's elders felt he was ready for his first battle. Lord Kato Kiyomasa ordered his ninjas to raid Udo Castle, which was controlled by his rival, Konishi Yukinaga.

YAAAA!

We have a long journey ahead of us. This will be a deadly battle, but we will emerge victorious!

Hanzō and the other shinobi warriors arrived at Udo Castle well after dark. Expecting a violent battle, they carried weapons such as *katanas* and *shuriken*.

Prepare to strike. We have the element of surprise!

Young Hanzō, come forward.

Your time is now, Hanzō. Your skill and courage will serve you well in battle.

It is an honor. I will lay my life down for this mission if needed.

Hanzō's group of shinobi warriors was the first to reach the wall. They climbed the wall in silence—unsure of what awaited them on the other side.

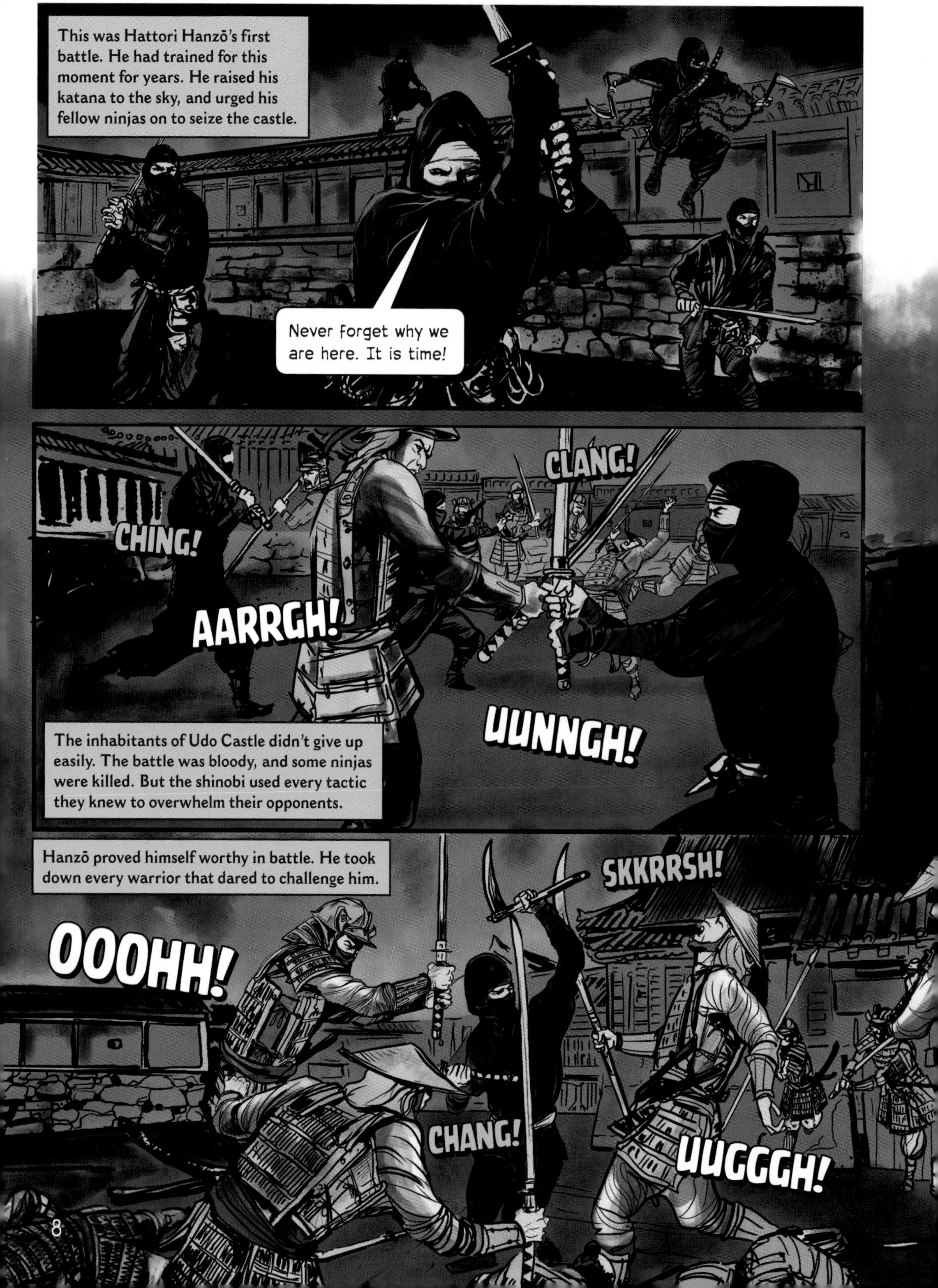
This was Hattori Hanzō's first battle. He had trained for this moment for years. He raised his katana to the sky, and urged his fellow ninjas on to seize the castle.
Never forget why we are here. It is time!
CLANG!
CHING!
AARRGH!
UUNNGH!
The inhabitants of Udo Castle didn't give up easily. The battle was bloody, and some ninjas were killed. But the shinobi used every tactic they knew to overwhelm their opponents.
Hanzō proved himself worthy in battle. He took down every warrior that dared to challenge him.
SKKRRSH!
OOOHH!
CHANG!
UUGGGH!

For his fierceness in battle, Hanzō was given the nickname "Demon Hanzō." He was also presented with a special weapon from shōgun Tokugawa Ieyasu, Japan's military leader.

You have earned the respect of these men . . . and of me. Use my demon-killing spear well.

Thank you, Ieyasu. I will cherish it and use it to claim victory in every mission.

Following the victory at Udo Castle, Hanzō became a leader of the shinobi. He trained the next generation of warriors and led them into many more battles.

A katana is your best weapon, but it requires you to be close to your enemy. Learn the shuriken and you can eliminate your enemy before he ever sees you.

Follow me and you shall grow to be the finest shinobi in the land!

SARUTOBI'S DEADLY MISSION

Kozuki Sasuke was another legendary ninja in feudal Japan. Stories of his achievements were passed down through several generations. Over time, tales of Sasuke's adventures evolved into stories about a ninja named Sarutobi Sasuke. Sarutobi is a popular character in many fictional stories. However, his abilities and achievements are based on Kozuki Sasuke and other ninjas of the time.

Like Kozuki, Sarutobi was deadly with a spear called a *yari*. Sarutobi practiced his fighting skills daily, but his biggest talent was acting as a spy.

Sarutobi, come to me!

Sarutobi, you have mastered the yari and are the fastest I've ever seen. You are an expert at evading the enemy and your skills as a spy are impressive.

Thank you, master. I am honored to serve you.

Go and rest now. Come to me at dawn. I have a mission for you.

You will go to the castle of the shōgun and act as my spy.

Yes, master.

The shōgun believes I am disloyal. I fear he has plans to do me harm. You will find out the truth. Go at once.

It was a long journey to the castle of the shōgun. Sarutobi moved through the treetops to avoid being seen by his enemies. They expected an attack from the ground and would be looking for footprints.

I must sneak into the castle and learn what they have planned for my master.

Ninjas had many tools for climbing. Sarutobi used the *musubi bashigo*. It was a rope ladder made for scaling high walls.

Almost over the wall and the guards have no idea I'm here. Fools! This will be an easy mission!

One of a ninja's most valuable tools was a *saoto hikigane*. This cone-shaped device allowed ninjas to listen to conversations without being seen.

He cannot be trusted. Gather your men and travel to him in the morning. I want him eliminated.

I must warn the Master.

Consider it done, Lord.

As he was preparing to leave, two guards spotted Sarutobi creeping along the top of the wall. The guards were no match for his speed and agility. He was over the wall before they could catch him.

We will hunt you down and it will be the end of you!

But Sarutobi landed in a bear trap on the other side of the wall. His foot was badly injured.

AAAAGGGHH!

They'll find me here and are certain to kill me. I need to free myself!

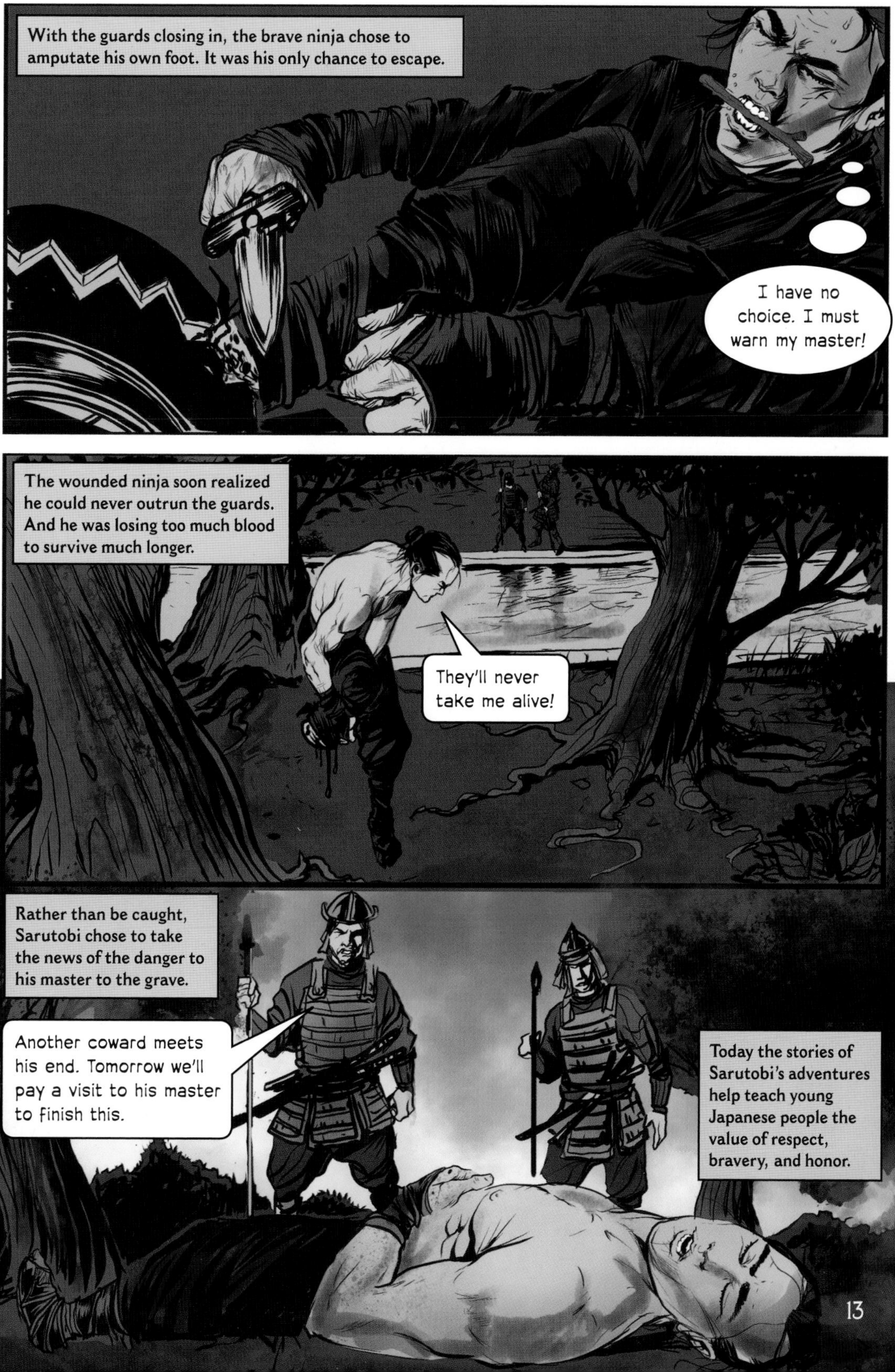
With the guards closing in, the brave ninja chose to amputate his own foot. It was his only chance to escape.
I have no choice. I must warn my master!
The wounded ninja soon realized he could never outrun the guards. And he was losing too much blood to survive much longer.
They'll never take me alive!
Rather than be caught, Sarutobi chose to take the news of the danger to his master to the grave.
Another coward meets his end. Tomorrow we'll pay a visit to his master to finish this.
Today the stories of Sarutobi's adventures help teach young Japanese people the value of respect, bravery, and honor.

FŪMA KOTARŌ, NINJA GIANT

One of the most feared ninjas of all time was Fūma Kotarō. He was the leader of the Fūma clan in the late 1500s. Legend says that Kotarō was a giant of a man who was bigger and stronger than any of his men. The Fūma clan fought many battles against the rival Takeda group. Each side tried to drive the other out and take control of the territory.

My patience is gone. The Takeda must be destroyed. Their camp is at Ukishimagahara. We must begin training immediately!

The Fūma clan practiced guerilla warfare. They often used surprise attacks and unusual strategies in combat. One of their tactics was to blind enemies with hollow eggs, called *hai lan*. The ninjas blew the egg out of its shell, then filled the empty shell with toxic dust or ashes.

One strike to your enemy's face and they'll be blinded. Then you can finish them with your sword!

The Fūma clan planned to attack at night and surprise the enemy with silent weapons. The *fukiya* looked like a common flute. But it was a deadly blowgun that could shoot poison darts and kill a man from 20 feet (6 meters) away.

FWIP!

FWIP!

We'll hit their horses first with the poison darts. This will cause a panic. Then when the Takeda run from their huts, we will strike!

Continue to practice. You must be able to hit your target from a great distance. You cannot miss—the mission depends on it!

We will set up camp tonight upriver from the Takeda and strike at midnight.

Victory will be ours!

The *bo shuriken* were small weapons that ninjas could easily hide. When thrown correctly, the sharp blades were deadly.

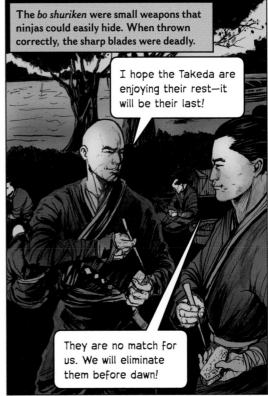

I hope the Takeda are enjoying their rest—it will be their last!

They are no match for us. We will eliminate them before dawn!

The stealthy ninjas closed in on the camp. Many hid behind trees and waited for Kotarō's signal to shoot their deadly darts at the enemy's horses.

Kōgeki! Kōgeki!
(Attack! Attack!)

15

The Takeda were helpless against an invisible enemy. Poison darts and bo shuriken flew everywhere. Takeda warriors couldn't see their attackers. But they grew desperate and began fighting in the darkness.

FWIP!

FWIP!

AAGGH!

FWIP!

Fire back, men! Shoot at the darkness and silence the ghost enemy!

UUGGGH!

FWIP!

AAGGH!

FWIP!

CLANG!

NOOO!

UUNNG!

The guerilla tactics of the Fūma clan confused the Takeda. Unsure who was attacking, they attacked anything that moved. Stories say that many were killed by members of their own clan.

The fools don't even know who they're attacking! They're killing each other! Our plan is working.

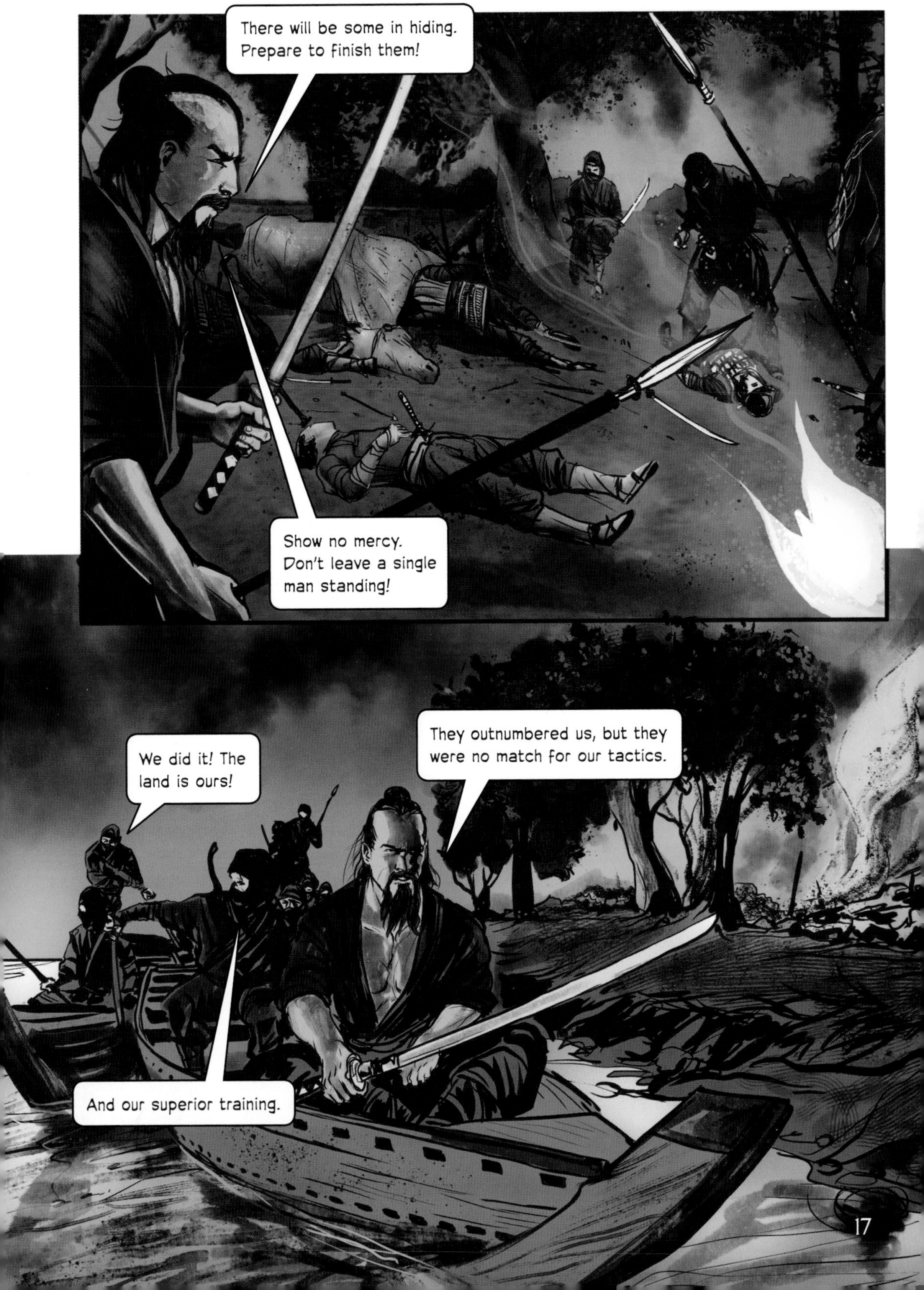
There will be some in hiding. Prepare to finish them!
Show no mercy. Don't leave a single man standing!
We did it! The land is ours!
They outnumbered us, but they were no match for our tactics.
And our superior training.

KUNOICHI, FIERCE FEMALE WARRIORS

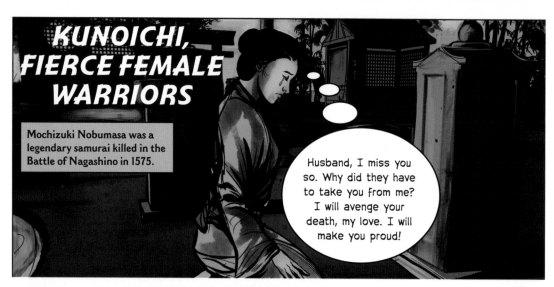

Mochizuki Nobumasa was a legendary samurai killed in the Battle of Nagashino in 1575.

Husband, I miss you so. Why did they have to take you from me? I will avenge your death, my love. I will make you proud!

After Nobumasa died his wife, Mochizuki Chiyome, went to live with her late-husband's uncle, Takeda Shingen. Takeda was a powerful feudal lord.

Welcome, child. Come in and be safe. I will care for you in your time of mourning.

Many thanks, Takeda. I am forever grateful.

Mochizuki had been married to a samurai, but she had ninja roots. She came from the Koga clan and stories say that Takeda had plans for her.

You are a warrior princess at heart. You can be a great leader in battle.

What do you mean, Takeda? I am no leader!

But you are. You can be very useful to me. I want you to gather and train a band of female ninja warriors!

At Takeda's request, Mochizuki gathered a group of mostly poor, uneducated women from the streets.

I have chosen you because you have greatness inside of you. I believe in you, and I will train you to be ninja warriors!

Yes! Thank you!

We are ready!

This is your katana. I will train you to be stealthy and avoid fights. But you must be prepared to defend yourself—or die!

Ninjas used many types of weapons. Learning to use each was important to be successful.

The *shinobi-zue* was one of the ninjas' best weapons. These hollow walking sticks had many uses.

The shinobi-zue is your most important weapon. Keep it with you at all times.

With this one tool, you can deliver a deadly poison dart, strike an enemy, or hide underwater for hours.

19

Tales say that the female ninjas trained under Mochizuki Chiyome for months. They learned the art of evasion, and they became master spies. They also learned how to defeat their enemy in hand-to-hand combat.

Are you ready to prove yourselves worthy warriors?

We are ready!

Good! Your training is almost complete.

With their training complete, the women were officially *Kunoichi*. They were ninjas.

You came from the streets. You were abandoned and unwanted. But now you are the most powerful women in the land! You are ready!

The Kunoichi were sent out on many missions. Sometimes they pretended to be dancers. But they acted as spies to get secret information.

She dances very well, this one. So graceful and elegant.

Enjoy the show you foolish pigs.

The Kunoichi usually worked alone. But sometimes they worked together to carry out a mission. One Kunoichi would serve undercover as a *geisha*, or entertainer. She distracted the men of the house, allowing her partners to secretly gather information without being seen.

Your beauty is remarkable. After dinner, you will dance for me.

It would be my honor to dance for you, my emperor.

The scrolls are in the emperor's chambers. We must retrieve them and get them to Mochizuki.

Such foolish men. This mission will be easy!

You have done well for your first mission. You make me proud.

You trained us well, Mochizuki. We owe our lives to you.

There will be many more missions in your future. You will be remembered as the greatest Kunoichi in the land!

21

THE FALL OF THE IGA

Iga province was a mountainous region in southern Japan. It was home to one of the largest ninja clans. Many people believe Iga was the birthplace of ninjutsu.

The Oda clan was a powerful family of feudal lords. They grew their empire by conquering other clans and taking their land. They had a plan to defeat the ninjas and take over the Iga province.

We must continue to train. Lord Oda Nobunaga's son wants to take our land. We must be prepared to defend it to the death!

We will crush them!

Ninjas were trained to use special *hankyu* bows and *ya* arrows. They were small compared to regular bows and arrows. A ninja could easily carry the weapons in a bamboo tube on his back.

Yes!

Another valuable tool for the ninja was the *kusari-fundo*. Ninjas could use this heavy weighted chain to attack an enemy at close range. The ninjas of Iga province were experts at disarming enemies with the kusari-fundo.

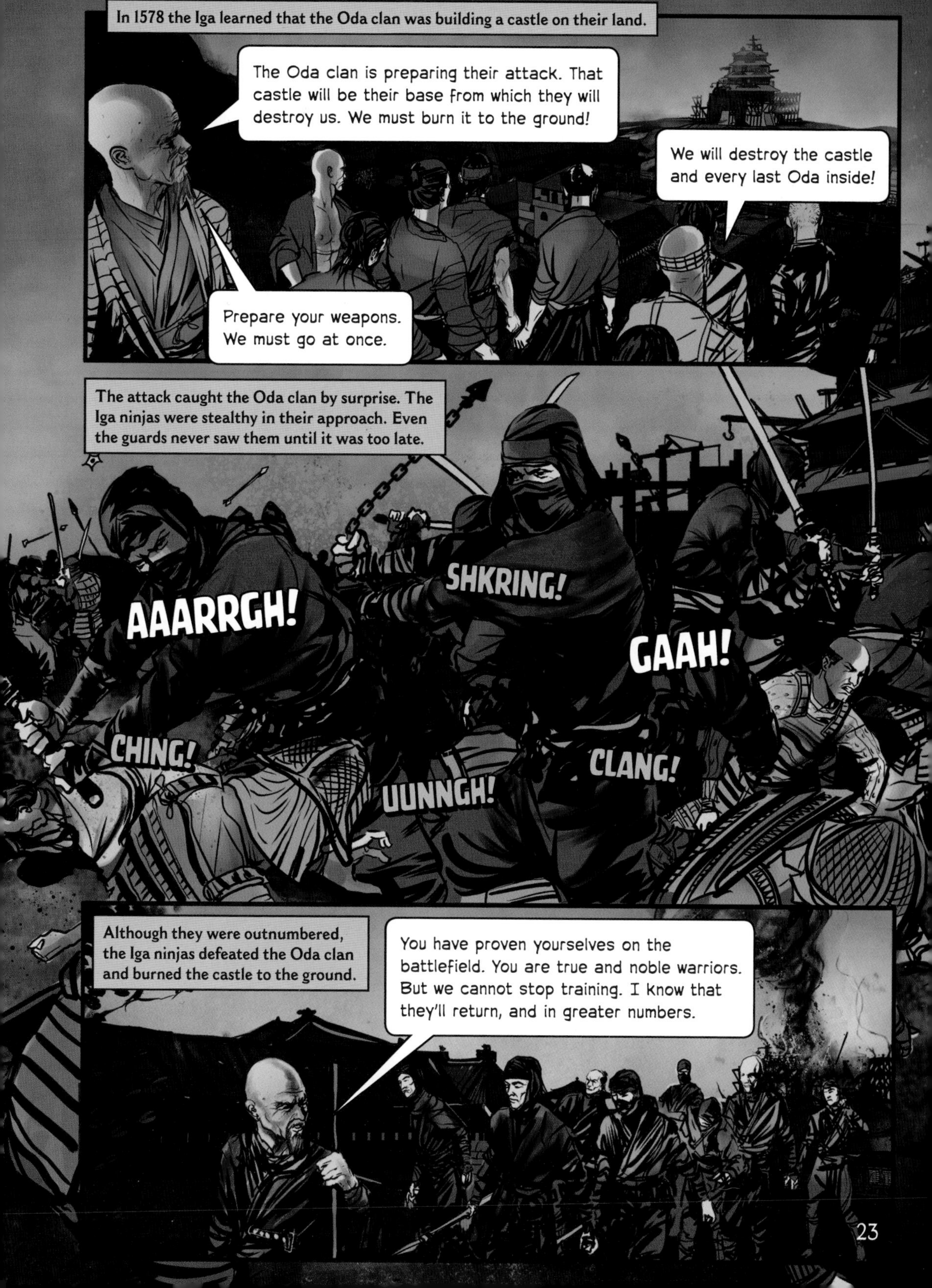
In 1578 the Iga learned that the Oda clan was building a castle on their land.
The Oda clan is preparing their attack. That castle will be their base from which they will destroy us. We must burn it to the ground!
We will destroy the castle and every last Oda inside!
Prepare your weapons. We must go at once.
The attack caught the Oda clan by surprise. The Iga ninjas were stealthy in their approach. Even the guards never saw them until it was too late.
SHKRING!
AAARRGH!
GAAH!
CHING!
CLANG!
UUNNGH!
Although they were outnumbered, the Iga ninjas defeated the Oda clan and burned the castle to the ground.
You have proven yourselves on the battlefield. You are true and noble warriors. But we cannot stop training. I know that they'll return, and in greater numbers.

Lord Oda Nobunaga was angered at his son's defeat at the hands of the Iga warriors. He decided to personally lead the return to Iga province. The Oda clan returned on October 1, 1581, for the second battle.

The Iga are weak. Their numbers are small. Now we will claim what is ours!

Nobunaga led an army of more than 40,000 Oda warriors. The Iga ninjas numbered only 4,000 men.

They may outnumber us, but this is *our* land.

If they want our land, they will need to spill all of our blood to get it!

The second battle of Iga province had a very different result. With superior forces and a strategic battle plan, the Oda clan quickly took the hill. Thousands of Iga ninjas were killed.

FWIP!

FWIP!

CHANG!

AAYYAAAH!

AAARGGH!

SHKRING!

OOOWW!

ZZZING!

24

We have avenged our earlier defeat! The blood of our brothers was not wasted. Iga province is ours!

Our empire is stronger than ever! We cannot be defeated!

They have taken our homeland and killed our people. We are all that is left. What should we do?

There is nothing to do but leave. They have our weapons, our dead, and our land.

The few Iga ninjas that survived the attack spread out across Japan.

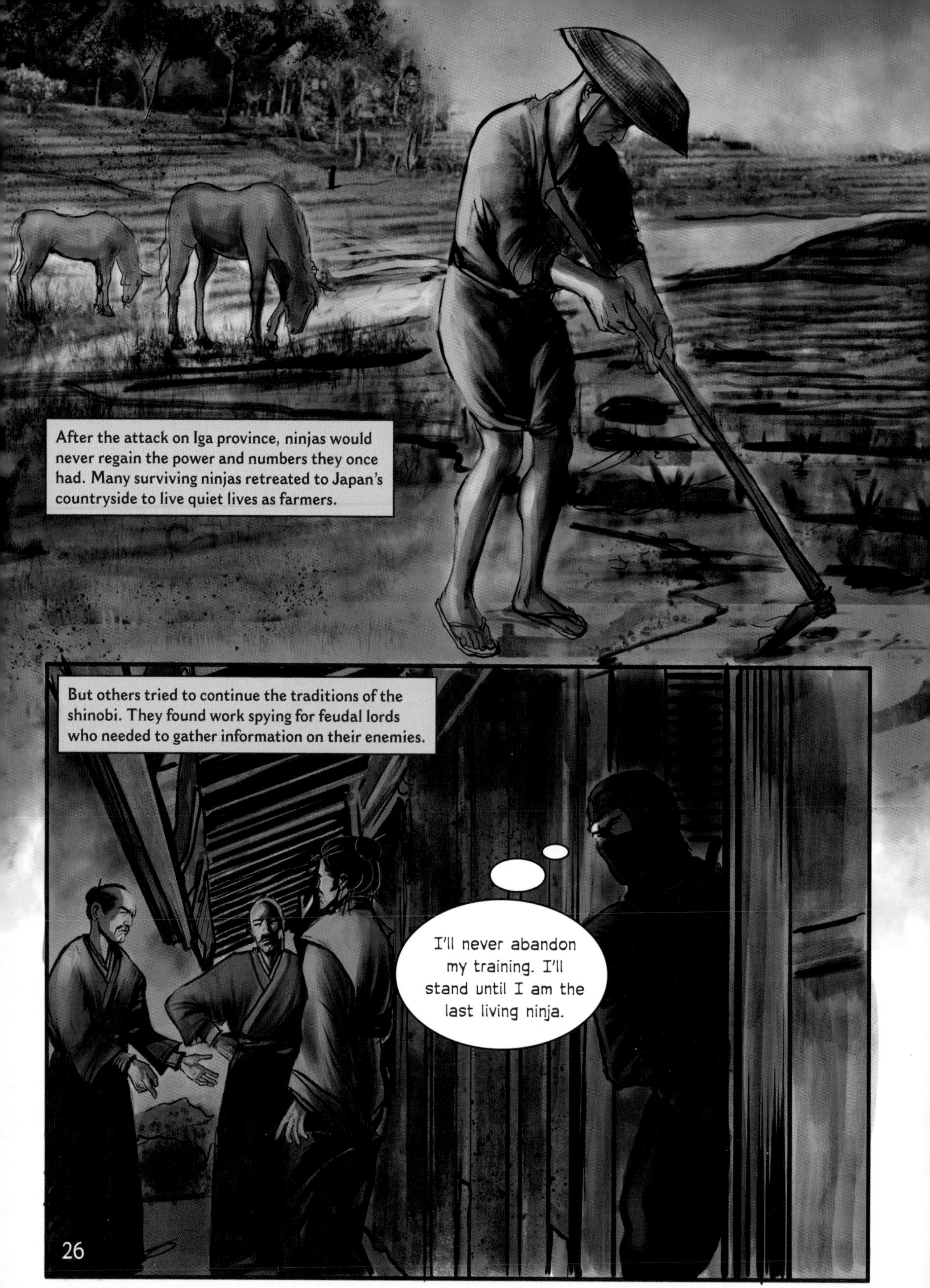
After the attack on Iga province, ninjas would never regain the power and numbers they once had. Many surviving ninjas retreated to Japan's countryside to live quiet lives as farmers.
But others tried to continue the traditions of the shinobi. They found work spying for feudal lords who needed to gather information on their enemies.
I'll never abandon my training. I'll stand until I am the last living ninja.

A few ninjas wanted to keep their traditions alive. They tried to teach a new generation of shinobi warriors.

There is great honor in the work we do. We are skilled in many things, and our traditions must live on!

But young people didn't want to be ninjas. Japan held new opportunities, and the danger of ninja life was too great.

Today, ninjas are a large part of popular culture. They are seen in movies, comic books, and TV shows. Ninjas are often shown using supernatural powers, such as walking on water and reading minds. These ideas came from old Japanese folktales told by people who feared ninjas and what they could do.

**DOUBLE FEATURE:
AMERICAN NINJA AND NINJA ASSASSIN
7pm SHOW TIME**

But real ninjas were ordinary people who were trained to do extraordinary things. Now, 400 years later, they remain an important part of Japan's rich history.

27

MORE ABOUT NINJAS

1

1558: Hattori Hanzō leads his first battle, the attack on Udo castle, at just 16 years old.

2

1575: Samurai Mochizuki is killed in the Battle of Nagashino. Following his death, his wife, Mochizuki Chiyome, forms a band of female Kunoichi ninjas to carry on his legacy.

3

1579: First Iga War is fought. The Iga province ninjas are victorious and save their land.

4

1581: Second Iga War is fought. The Oda clan outnumbers the Iga ninjas 10 to one and achieves total victory.

5

1581: Battle of Ukishimagahara. Fūma Kotarō leads a band of ninjas on a guerilla attack on the Takeda group. Kotarō is victorious in a bloody battle.

6

1590: The Hōjō ninja clan is defeated by Toyotomi Hideyoshi following the siege of Odawara Castle.

IMPORTANT EVENTS IN NINJA HISTORY

NINJA WEAPONS

Ninjas were trained mainly as spies. But they were also experts with many weapons. From swords and bows to secret, hidden blades, ninjas were deadly fighters if discovered by their enemies.

HANKYU

These short bows could be easily carried on a ninja's back while on missions. The bows shot bamboo arrows called ya.

KATANA

A traditional Japanese sword with a blade about 20 inches (51 centimeters) long. Ninjas wore these swords slung over their backs for ease while running and climbing.

SHURIKEN

Today these sharp blades are known as "throwing stars." Originally, the shuriken was a single small blade that could be hidden easily. Ninjas could quickly pull them out to throw at an enemy. There were said to be more than 350 types of shuriken.

NEKKOTE

These razor-sharp weapons were worn over a ninja's fingers. They acted like claws to cut an enemy during hand-to-hand combat. Ninjas sometimes dipped the claws in poison.

GLOSSARY

agility (uh-JIL-uh-tee)—the ability to move quickly and easily

amputate (AM-pyuh-tayt)—to cut off a person's arm, leg, or other body part, usually because of severe injuries

assassin (uh-SA-suhn)—a person who murders an important person, such as a president

avenge (uh-VENJ)—to get revenge on someone for an offense

evade (ih-VADE)—to escape or avoid capture

feudal (FYOOD-uhl)—relating to a system in which common people lived and worked on land that was owned by wealthy nobles

geisha (GEI-shaw)—a Japanese girl or woman who is trained to provide entertainment and company

guerilla warfare (guh-RIL-uh WOR-fair)—a type of military action using small groups of fighters to carry out surprise attacks against enemy forces

mourn (MORN)—to be very sad and miss someone who has died

ninjutsu (nihn-JIHT-soo)—martial arts skills practiced by ninjas

samurai (SAH-muh-rye)—a special class of warriors who fought for local lords in ancient Japan

shōgun (SHOH-gun)—a military general who once ruled Japan

READ MORE

Lusted, Marcia Amidon. *Ninja Science: Camouflage, Weapons and Stealthy Attacks.* Warrior Science. North Mankato, Minn.: Capstone Press, 2017.

Matthews, Rupert. *Ninjas.* History's Fearless Fighters. New York: Gareth Stevens Publishing, 2016.

Shaffer, Jody Jensen. *Ninja Warriors.* Ancient Warriors. Mankato, Minn: Child's World, 2015.

———

CRITICAL THINKING QUESTIONS

- Ninjas are famous for their stealthy skills and ability to avoid detection. Why are these important traits for ninjas? How did these skills help them survive?

- This book uses narration, dialogue, and illustrated art to tell stories about great ninjas. How do these elements work together to help you understand each story?

- The importance of honor is a theme throughout the book. What is one example of a great sacrifice that a ninja is willing to make for honor?

INTERNET SITES

Use Facthound to find Internet sites related to this book.

Visit *www.facthound.com*

Just type in 9781543555035 and go.

INDEX